The Complete String Guide:
Standards, Programs, Purchase, and Maintenance

The Complete String Guide:
Standards, Programs, Purchase, and Maintenance

A joint publication of:
American String Teachers Association
Music Educators National Conference
National School Orchestra Association

Copyright © 1988 by the Music Educators National Conference
1902 Association Drive, Reston, Virginia 22091
All rights reserved.
ISBN 0-940796-38-4

TABLE OF CONTENTS

Preface vii
Statement of philosophy ix
Introduction xi

Part I
    The importance of the string and orchestra program 2
    Why strings? 4
    Building and sustaining a high-quality string program 6
    When should strings be started? 9

Part II
    General care of instruments and bows 20
    Stringed instrument and equipment checklist 24

Part III
    Construction features of instruments 26
    Bridge curvatures and string heights 29

Part IV
    Writing specifications 36
    Checking your purchase 44

Appendix
    Nomenclature 48
    Stringed instrument size chart 50
    Summary of instrument materials and construction 51

PREFACE

The joint committee of ASTA, MENC, and NSOA that prepared this guide wishes to express its appreciation to the members of the MENC Ad Hoc Committee on Updating the Minimum Standards for Stringed Instruments for their contributions in the initial stages of the guide. Ad Hoc Committee members were G. Jean Smith (chair), Jacquelyn Dillon, and Jerry Kupchynsky.

In developing this guide, the joint committee of ASTA, MENC, and NSOA has not only made available what it intends as a useful, practical document for string teachers and orchestra directors; it also has established a precedent for cooperation among all string organizations in planning and developing instructional materials for teaching strings. All educational string organizations have a common goal—"improving and assisting in the development of string programs and orchestras wherever or in whatever stage they may be." By working together in such endeavors, we can be a more effective force in promoting string instruction in our schools.

Robert H. Klotman
Committee Chair
MENC Past-President, 1976–1978

Joint ASTA, MENC, and NSOA Committee

Robert Klotman, committee chair, professor emeritus of music, Indiana University, Bloomington

Charles Avsharian, president, Shar Products

Don Beene, music coordinator and director of orchestras, Los Alamos Schools, New Mexico

Sandy Dackow, supervisor of music, New Jersey Schools, Ridgewood

Kurt Glaesel, violin maker and general manager of Glaesel Strings, division of Selmer Company

Ed Siennicki, composer and former orchestra director in the Cleveland Public Schools

Pamela Tellejohn, orchestra coordinator, Richland County School District Two, Columbia, South Carolina

Photo by Robin Layton

STATEMENT OF PHILOSOPHY

Music education in the public schools exists for the purpose of awakening and refining the aesthetic sensitivities of all children. The instrumental music program should develop music skills, understandings, and attitudes that will enable students to enjoy a richer life through listening to or participating in music experiences.

No instrumental program can be considered complete unless it includes an orchestra program. A vast cultural heritage of man's artistic achievement in music lies within this genre. To ignore it is overlooking an area of one's humanistic, artistic, and intellectual education. All children should be provided with opportunities to pursue their interests and proclivities. Any school professing to have a balanced instrumental program must offer instruction in *all* of the traditional instruments, including strings.

Rehearsal activities in the instrumental music program should provide a conceptual understanding of the basic properties of melody, harmony, rhythm, dynamics, and form to help students become proficient on the instrument. It is the responsibility of administrators and music educators to implement a sequential plan of learning experiences that will meet the needs of all children so they can experience the musical growth needed to provide them with a means of self-expression.

Photo by Jack Pingel

INTRODUCTION

This is a joint publication of the American String Teachers Association (ASTA), the Music Educators National Conference (MENC), and the National School Orchestra Association (NSOA).

Dear Music Educator:

I have played cello for a number of years, and music remains an important part of my life. I am hopeful that young people today will enjoy the same opportunity I had, to work toward mastery of a stringed instrument. I believe that orchestral programs in our schools can play a part in helping all students gain an appreciation of great music.

I salute your dedication to providing balanced musical programs in our schools.

> Richard Lugar
> United States Senator
> (R, Indiana)

PART I

THE IMPORTANCE OF THE STRING AND ORCHESTRA PROGRAM

To offer a complete music program in the school curriculum, an orchestra should be included with all other instrumental and vocal programs. Too many school music offerings have excluded strings at the expense of the children entitled to these experiences. I am delighted to see our affiliated string and orchestra organizations join hands with MENC to produce a guide that will provide direction in improving this situation in our schools and society.

Donald L. Corbett
MENC President

In its 1986 publication *The School Music Program: Description and Standards*, MENC takes the position that both a "basic" and a "quality" school music program must include instruction in stringed instruments and an orchestra experience at the junior and senior high school levels.

Basic Program	Quality Program
General music is offered daily to each student in grades K-6. Instruction on band and orchestra instruments is offered beginning in grades four or five.*	General music is offered daily to to each student in grades K-6. Instruction on band and orchestra instruments, guitar, and keyboard instruments is offered beginning in grades four or five.* Exploratory instrumental classes are offered beginning no later than grade three. Choral experiences are offered beginning in grade five.
Orchestra or string orchestra is offered in both the high school and the junior high or middle school.	Full orchestra is offered in both the high school and the junior high or middle school. An additional orchestra ensemble is offered for each 300 students above 300 in the school.

---

*The committee recommends that instruction should be offered beginning in grades four, five, or six.

In 1973 the American Association of School Administrators (AASA) took the following stand regarding a balanced curriculum:

> As school budgets today come under extreme fiscal pressures, trimming or eliminating so-called "peripheral" subject areas from the school curriculum appears often to be a financially attractive economy.
>
> The American Association of School Administrators believes that a well-rounded, well-balanced curriculum is essential in the education of American children. We believe that deleting entire subject areas that have value in the total life experience of the individual is short-sighted.
>
> Therefore, AASA recommends that school administrators declare themselves in favor of maintaining a full, balanced curriculum at all grade levels, opposing any categorical cuts in the school program.

The American Association of School Administrators adopted this resolution February 25, 1973, at their annual business meeting and convention in Atlantic City, New Jersey. With AASA's permission, MENC has reprinted the resolution in the interest of furthering a well-balanced curriculum.

WHY STRINGS?

In view of the previous endorsements, it seems most incongruous that students in schools across the nation usually have the opportunity to participate in classroom music and choral and band programs, but only those in selected districts have access to string instruction and orchestra programs.

Each student is entitled to the opportunity to explore classroom music activities, vocal activities, and the study of a band or orchestra instrument during his or her public school career. Orchestra activities are just as important as band or choral activities, and they do not require any greater financial commitment or administrative responsibilities.

In addition to the school orchestra, many activities for stringed instrument performances exist: solo recitals, district and state solo and ensemble contests, various ensemble formats, string orchestras, chamber orchestras, orchestra festivals, musical production pit orchestras, youth symphonies, and summer music camp orchestras.

The orchestra's literature is one of Western culture's great treasures. It is familiar to the average listener. A school orchestra is not only of value to its participants; it is an asset to the school and community as well. Those who view school music in terms of content as well as process and activity cannot help but be impressed by the literature that an orchestra program brings to its members and audience.

Many students prefer the sound of an orchestra to that of a band and would rather participate in an orchestra program than a marching band program. These students are attracted to the sound of stringed instruments or the music written for strings. In addition, orchestra and string literature reflects a broader historical perspective than one finds in other instrumental literature. For this reason, some parents will encourage their child to play a stringed instrument if the opportunity exists.

It is important to remember that a school music program without orchestra activities seriously shortchanges not only those individuals who wish to study a stringed instrument, but it also limits woodwind, brass, percussion, and vocal students. Orchestra opportunities for woodwind, brass, and percussion performers provide solo responsibilities not common in a typical band program and develop increased musicianship. Furthermore, without strings, the masterworks for chorus and orchestra can only be performed with keyboard instruments. Musical theater productions cannot be produced without hiring outside string players. Denying the opportunity to perform orchestra music hampers full musical development of any player. According to MENC's *The School Music Program: Description and Standards*, the musical life of any school cannot be considered of good or even basic quality without an orchestra.

Many schools and communities support an orchestra program for utilitarian reasons, including memorial services, graduation ceremonies, and civic group performances. Music productions and performances of joint choral and orchestra works are popular with communities that support orchestra programs. Opportunities for playing stringed instruments abound. According to the American Symphony Orchestra League, adults in this country have access to 1,650 orchestras, as well as uncounted smaller groups such as quartets or trios. Furthermore, through participation in school programs, string players and other orchestra members can be exposed to orchestra literature at a very influential period in their lives when lasting values are being formed.

Playing a stringed instrument integrates a person's physical, intellectual, and expressive qualities. For many individuals, the study of a stringed instrument provides the most direct means of combining hands, head, and heart.

Contrary to popular misconceptions, stringed instruments are easily taught because the technical problems regarding the physical production of the tone are observable; they are visible to both learner and teacher. This insight should not be confused with the fact that progress in the beginning stages may seem to be slow since there are many skills that need to be developed.

Those citing many excuses for the lack of orchestra activity in a school district need only observe the variety of successful string and orchestra programs in all parts of the country where a commitment has been made to their success. Programs have been successfully initiated (with impressive results) in all types of geographic locations under a variety of demographic and socioeconomic circumstances. The key ingredient seems to be an administration's willingness to make a commitment to the program's success combined with an appropriate schedule, adequate funds, and properly trained and enthusiastic teachers.

BUILDING AND SUSTAINING A HIGH-QUALITY STRING PROGRAM

How does one develop a *high-quality* string program so that it benefits students, school, and community? Certain ingredients are integral to a successful string program. They will vary in strength depending on the quality of the teacher's enthusiasm, training, and experience and on community variables such as the availability of good private teachers. The following ingredients seem to exist where successful programs flourish:

- *The hiring of string personnel who have a strong background in string performance and who possess a desire to teach and a commitment to teaching.* Successful programs can be taught by instrumental teachers (who are not string majors) who are sufficiently capable and trained to teach strings. Ideally, however, a string teacher is preferable whenever possible. Teachers should maintain their performance skills by continuing their study of all stringed instruments, attending master classes, performing in community ensembles or orchestras, and participating in recitals and chamber music. They should be active in their professional organizations, attending meetings and assisting in local, district, and state activities such as solo and ensemble contests and all-state arrangements. They also should possess a strong commitment to the development of student interests and abilities.

- *The establishment of long-range goals for the recruitment of students, scheduling of classes, building of a library, and development of performance opportunities.* All students should have an equal opportunity to learn to play a stringed instrument. The recruitment process should be used to attract all students who would benefit from the program, including those who have a strong piano background, "good" ears, leadership ability, and good classroom work habits. To identify these students, one should involve and consult with the classroom teacher and general music teacher to determine the students' interests and music potential. It is important, however, that all interested children have the opportunity to participate in the program and that no student be excluded because of music test scores or economic difficulties. A demonstration by upper-level string students is an effective tool. Other recruitment demonstration options include performances or presentations by either faculty members or a demonstration team provided by a local music dealer. Another method would be to set up a summer exploratory program that permits students to try the various instruments before selecting one. This sort of activity could be incorporated into the general music class. String classes should be scheduled regularly during the school day. An ideal program would include a minimum of twice-weekly elementary school lessons and daily orchestra periods at the junior high and high school levels. Ensemble classes should be offered, and time for individual assistance should be available at all levels. Sectional rehearsals and small ensembles are a vital part of the curriculum.

- *The establishment of a budget item for repair and purchase of school-owned stringed instruments.* Because stringed instruments do not wear out as quickly as band instruments, the major costs are the initial purchase and the yearly maintenance for such items as rehairing the bow, replacing the strings and bridge, and repairing rough edges and marred finishes. When developing a music library, one should include small ensemble, string, and full orchestra music. Attention should be given to the purchase of music from different periods, styles, and technical levels. Graded state lists from state organizations and other sources can be of great help when purchasing music. It is most important that damaged music is repaired or replaced following its use. A card catalog cross-indexed by composer and title is helpful. A computer indexing system should be used.

- *The purchase of cellos, string basses, and violas with school funds to ensure a well-balanced program at all levels of instruction.* Some communities may also need to purchase small-sized instruments and some violins.

- *The maintenance of excellent programming that includes solo opportunities and the use of high-quality literature that includes both string and full orchestra compositions.* Establish a series of student recitals at the school, and encourage local arts councils or music clubs to sponsor them. Contact civic organizations for performance opportunities. Provide solos and ensembles for various school functions. A select chamber orchestra can be developed out of the concert orchestra. *Students need and want to perform.* There is much string literature available that is musically worthwhile but not technically difficult. Always program some music that challenges the student. It has been proven in many educational studies that one gets what one expects from students. Do not underestimate their desire to perform good music and their ability to grow to your level of expectation.

- *The encouragement of students to study with private teachers as they progress.* Individual attention is a vital part of the student's development. Class lessons and large group performances are important, but they do not always provide the individual attention necessary for full development of all playing techniques. Training in positions, shifting, vibrato development, intonation, rhythmic precision, bow control, and articulation is beneficial to the student. There is a wealth of excellent string solo literature to be explored as musical artistry and self-expression grow. Individual instruction will enhance a student's technical and musical growth in these areas.

- *The expectation that parents will purchase good-quality, full-sized violins, violas, and cellos.* This financial investment leads to an investment of time, interest, and effort to ensure the success of their children, and, in turn, the success of the school program. Practice habits, attitudes, and skills improve when students own their instruments. Most music instrument dealers will support your program with excellent "rent to purchase" plans. Initially, students may rent instruments, particularly small-sized ones. Many of these rental contracts contain an unlimited rental clause that enables the renter to upgrade the equipment as the child grows. As your string community becomes accustomed to purchasing instruments, the members will develop a "buy, sell, and trade" practice among themselves.

- *The expectation of high performance standards for all.* Private lessons, along with the use of section rehearsals, small ensembles, and selected performance groups, can help you realize performance goals. Encourage students to participate in solo opportunities and all-state or district festivals and to attend summer music camps, workshops by guests artists and clinicians, and master classes. All of these activities contribute toward higher performance standards.

WHEN SHOULD STRINGS BE STARTED?

Although stringed instrument instruction can begin at any age, most school string programs start in fourth, fifth, or sixth grade. In establishing a public or private school program, several questions should be asked:

- *What is the structure of the overall school system (K-5, K-6, 6-8, 7-9, and so forth)?* If the sixth grade is in a middle school, you can avoid scheduling and academic conflicts by starting strings in the sixth grade. In this structure you do not have to take students out of academic classes since students can take strings as a regular part of their schedule. If the sixth grade is still in the elementary school, you will have to decide whether to take students out of academic classes or wait and start beginners in the seventh grade. Although seventh grade is not too late to begin, it usually is difficult to get students interested at this age. Many students have already developed other interests, and the orchestra may not have as strong an appeal.

- *How many times per week can the class meet at each level?* Ideally, fourth- and fifth-grade string players should meet three to five times per week. This situation, however, is usually the exception and not the rule in today's schools. Therefore, if you can see the students three to five times per week at the sixth- grade level as opposed to one or two times per week at the fourth- or fifth- grade level, it would be advantageous to start at the sixth grade. The students will progress faster and maintain their interest longer, and the dropout rate will be drastically reduced. Although fewer students may start at an earlier age, the attrition rate for older beginners is much lower, and better results can be produced at the high school level.

- *What type of facilities are available?* Facilities are important. String teachers should not degrade their profession by agreeing to teach under poor conditions, such as in a small room or on a stage while lunch is being served on the other side of the curtain. Teaching in a regular classroom at a middle school is preferable to teaching in the janitor's closet at an elementary school. Thus, the type of facilities can influence the grade level at which you should start strings. Circumstances, however, may necessitate using one's imagination to find *temporary* housing if the opportunity to teach strings arises where none existed before.

- *Will the students have to be taken out of their regular classroom subjects to be in string class?* If so, you will always have difficulty. Some teachers are very enthusiastic, but others will never cooperate and may try to influence students not to take strings because they fear the extra class will lower students' grades in other subjects. If a program is structured so that you have no choice but to schedule students this way, then you must go out of your way to establish good public relations.

- *How many teachers are available to cover a certain number of schools?* Staff size can determine the number of grades to be started. Try to start as many students as possible at the same grade level so the program will be large. Do not start a few in the fourth grade, a few in the fifth grade, and a few in the sixth grade. By the time those students reach high school, there will not be enough students to create an orchestra, which will result in an image problem. It would be much more advantageous to start a larger number of students in the same grade level. If you start at two grade levels, however, make them consecutive (fifth and sixth, not fifth and seventh). Students who independently express interest in strings should be allowed to begin regardless of grade level. They can usually accelerate to the next class level by taking private lessons.

- *Should the band and orchestra program be started at the same time?* There are many advantages in starting the string program the same year as the band.
    1. The students choose from the beginning which group to be in. Rarely do students change their minds a year later.
    2. Fewer students may be involved than would have participated if the program had been started ahead of the band, but the dropout rate will be reduced.
    3. Since the dropout rate is lower, the negative image given to your program by students quitting or transferring to a wind instrument is practically eliminated.
    4. The band director will be more cooperative since he will have a fair chance at all students.
    5. More students will be interested in instrumental music because so many students are starting at the same time. It gives the impression that "everyone" is playing an instrument. Thus, many others join both programs. Students start thinking, "Which instrument should I play?" rather than "Should I play an instrument?" Both band and orchestra enrollments increase in this system.

Recruiting

There are many string teachers who advocate recruiting string players at an early age because they believe that it takes more time to develop a string player than it does a wind player. The choice of when to begin will depend on the school program and its philosophy regarding the total instrumental program. Whatever direction is selected for recruiting should be developed in conjunction with the entire program.

First and foremost, an excellent recruiting program depends on an excellent public image. This aspect of recruitment is discussed in the section on public relations (pages 11-15). All students should have an equal opportunity to learn to play a stringed instrument. Recruiting is not intended to eliminate any student. It is a program designed to attract those students to the string program who can be identified as particular candidates for success because of their musicality, leadership ability, and appropriate work habits.

Aptitude tests also may be used to identify potential string students. One should be especially careful in considering the validity of these tests, however. Actually, they can serve as a vehicle to open communications with candidates and their parents rather than a way to discover talent. They should not be used to discourage interested students.

Public relations

Thoughts about public relations and recruiting eventually involve publicity and advertising, which suggests communications (spreading the word). Many excellent articles have provided procedures for acquiring written or media publicity. In the business community the greatest publicity is achieved by word of mouth, which can be either positive or negative. Salespeople must educate consumers in order to sell to them. Educators need to sell potential consumers on the benefits of music in order to educate them. Selling or promoting means showing the consumers how they will benefit by acquiring an item or an idea. It is important that orchestra teachers provide opportunities for the community to enjoy the benefits of studying and listening to music. Spreading the word and recruiting is an ongoing process that begins with the first impression the teacher makes on the school or community and continues throughout the years.

To convince the public that playing an orchestra instrument is rewarding, the teacher needs to communicate the message to the community. To be successful, you must gain the respect and trust of potential consumers—you have to sell yourself before you can sell your product.

A music teacher working alone cannot build a successful orchestra program; help is needed. If you communicate your needs successfully, many people will be willing to help.

Teaching only the pupils who are assigned to orchestra is not sufficient. Enthusiastic music teachers try to extend their range of influence as far as possible to other pupils, music teachers, faculty members, administrators, parents, members of the school board, members of the community, and influential people who guide the community. There are no limits.

Pupils in the orchestra can be your best "missionaries." If students have positive and rewarding experiences, they will tell their friends, younger siblings, other relatives, and anyone else who will listen, and in future years they will be supportive adults of school and community music programs.

Pupils who are not in orchestra should not be neglected. Many will be in the audience during a music program. If the school orchestra only presents formal concerts, a good chance will be missed to teach the audience about orchestra music. The teacher who thinks of the concert as a demonstration rather than a formal ritual can point out various aspects of the performance ahead of time so that members of the audience can learn regardless of their level of musical background. Point out certain instruments, prominent players, how the music is put together, information about the composer, or the new instrument that was donated by the PTA or bought through the results of a fundraising drive. Do not hide your love and enthusiasm for music and people. Talk to the audience. Make the audience feel that you are happy that they attended the performance.

Make use of a display case or bulletin board near the music room to stimulate student interest. Displays of instruments, musicians, music notation for well-known songs ("name that tune"), holiday music, and music questions can create interest.

Other music teachers in the building should be your best allies. Be friendly, courteous, and appreciative of their good work. Tell them about it, or write notes to them expressing admiration for their work. Ask them for advice or help and talk about what is good for the members of the orchestra. Show an interest in the music classes that are not assigned to you; if you are sincere and friendly, others are more apt to respond in the same manner. A narrow view causes some teachers to compete with each other for a bigger piece of the pie. With a positive, cooperative approach and an enlarged percentage of the school population interested in music, the pie will be larger. Everyone will benefit (especially the children). There will be a great influence on a school and a community when music teachers work together to build an well-balanced music program. Successes and failures of other music teachers affect your successes and failures.

Without the good will of the rest of the faculty, chances for a successful music program are slim because of the nature of the subject. The music teacher has the potential for disrupting the school schedule more than any other teacher. How often are musicians excused from their regular classes for rehearsals, festivals, assemblies, or field trips? This upsets the work and planning of many teachers and causes them hardships. Music teachers need the support of fellow teachers. Therefore, friendship, courtesy, and appreciation for others is important. Show interest in the entire school and be an involved member of the faculty. Sincerely compliment other teachers for their good work. Visit other classes or homerooms. Be visible in the school building. When pupils need to be excused from string classes for projects, be flexible and, if possible, excuse them.

Without the support of administrators, the music program would have a difficult time. Administrators are interested in the education of all the schoolchildren. Present the string program message to the principal, assistant principal, schedule maker, and counselor in a manner that shows how the orchestra can be an asset to the entire school population. Meet with them whenever possible and keep them informed of your students' progress. Display interest in the entire school by being a member of school committees.

The support of nonteaching staff members can be very helpful. Office clerks may share information regarding funds that may be available for the string program. A friendly custodial staff can smooth the process when large pieces of equipment need to be moved. The person who is in charge of the office copy machine can be helpful, as can the individual in charge of the stage and the light board.

The goodwill of parents, relatives, and neighbors can influence an administrator's decisions about the music program. Courtesy, friendliness, and appreciation will go a long way in building a receptive audience. At concert demonstrations make sure all children onstage can be seen by their relatives in the audience. If conditions make this impossible, when acknowledging applause, have the back row of the orchestra stand first and continue until the entire orchestra is standing. Also, step aside so the children are receiving the applause; then bow as a gesture of thanks from the children to the audience.

It is sometimes desirable to program a piece at a concert demonstration for its entertainment value rather than for its musical value. This can attract less musically sophisticated people who are potential supporters of the orchestra program. Once they are in the audience, it is easier to show them how to appreciate music for its artistic merits as well as its entertainment value.

A teacher might be tempted to take the easy way out by programming only popular music and avoiding what is considered "good literature." By succumbing to this temptation, the teacher does not provide a good product and becomes a "store clerk" who packages an article and rings up the cash register for a person who decides what he wants before coming into the store.

School board members are as interested in children and the school as are parents and administrators. They also need to learn about the benefits of the school orchestra program.

Members of the community who have no official connection to the school are often interested in the school system. Contact with them may turn them into ambassadors for the music program. You may meet them when you provide musical services at their civic meetings and holiday festivities. Every person to whom the school's string story is told can turn out to be a walking, talking billboard for the children and for the orchestra program.

Political officeholders can be helpful, but do not overlook the other people who have influence in the community. Often they work quietly, shunning the spotlight, working for the good of the community. They are not easy to find. They could be bankers, store owners, business people, owners of large parcels of land, or any number of people who have invested in the community. Although they are busy with their interests, they know what is going on in the community, and often they are the decision makers. They should be made aware of the benefits of the orchestra program as it relates to the community.

If teachers are happy and enthusiastic about music and perform on their instrument at concerts, churches, parties, and other occasions, they will be displaying positive results of the benefits they received as members of their school orchestra programs when they were students.

In retrospect, public relations and recruiting are intertwined, and the burden for success falls upon the teacher alone—no one else. To be a good communicator, you need not be a glib, smooth-talking salesperson. In any business, attributes such as sincerity, friendliness, a concern for others, appropriate dress and appearance, dependability, social graces, a good telephone voice and manner, the ability to communicate, enthusiasm, a positive attitude, confidence, organizational ability, and an ongoing missionary zeal to have others learn about the benefits of your product are important. Attending conventions, workshops, and association meetings; reading trade journals and books on music; exchanging information with other teachers; and having a mentor

are excellent activities for growth. Since teaching is selling, reading a book or two each year about sales or marketing will sharpen your communication skills. Study the techniques used by salespeople to differentiate between good and bad performance. Books about making friends, positive thinking, successful people in the business world, and feeding the subconscious can be helpful for developing the craft of communication.

Many excellent articles have been written about publicity and recruiting; they should not be neglected. It is important to know how to write news releases, make recruiting forms, and contact radio and television stations. The catalysts for an excellent orchestra program are the communication skills and selling ability of the orchestra teacher.

Training string teachers

String teachers, like most other teachers, teach their subject matter much as they were taught. This cycle inhibits growth and progress. If string teaching is to be effective in the future, the profession must identify the essential competencies necessary for effective string teaching and design courses that will produce these competencies.

Although many colleges offer K-12 music certification, other colleges allow for more specialized instrumental, vocal, or classroom training or certification options. Some students may be equally interested and skilled in more than one area, but there are likely to be three types of candidates for music education certification: those with vocal emphasis; those with wind, percussion, or band emphasis; and those with string and orchestra emphasis.

At least two semesters of string methods should be required of all vocal education students. This ideally should be divided into one semester of violin and viola methods, followed by a second semester of cello and bass methods. These students also should be involved in two semesters of an instrumental methods course covering elementary, junior high, and high school orchestra materials, plus teaching and rehearsal techniques. This experience may or may not be coupled with a similar course on band methods and materials.

Courses that teach all four stringed instruments in a single semester are inadequate. No one can learn to play an instrument in one semester, but one semester on each family can provide fundamental techniques and skills necessary to teach and demonstrate pertinent aspects of the instruments. It would be far more significant to offer these classes in a sequence of heterogeneous class teaching. In many school situations, string instruction is taught under those conditions.

For the wind or percussion major choosing an instrumental music emphasis, four semesters of string study is preferable: two on violin, one on cello, and the fourth divided between viola and bass. In addition, this student also should take two semesters (preferably four) of an instrumental methods course dealing with materials and teaching strategies for elementary, junior high, and high school orchestra, string orchestra, and elementary chamber music. Both homogeneous (like instrument) and heterogeneous (full string class, full orchestra) materials and approaches should be included in the experience. If possible, wind or percussion majors should perform on their major instrument with the college orchestra at some point during their undergraduate study.

A music education student majoring in a stringed instrument who chooses to specialize in the string or orchestra area should follow the same basic curriculum as wind or percussion students, but should add at least two semesters of private applied study on an opposite-type stringed instrument (cello or bass for the violinist or violist and vice versa). Instead of the required two semesters of basic violin class, a separate course should be substituted for string majors involving an in-depth study of materials and philosophies of a variety of pedagogies. This course could overlap one meeting per week with the basic violin class so the string majors could act as teaching assistants. String majors should follow the same methods curriculum in woodwind, brass, and percussion areas as the wind or percussion majors. Experience in band methods and in conducting bands as well as choral experiences will greatly enhance the string major's effectiveness in dealing with full orchestras.

Skill levels for vocal education majors should encompass first-position chromatic ability on violin and viola, first position with extensions on cello, and half and first positions on bass; some experience and skill should also be required with third-position notes and shifts for violin and viola, fourth-position notes and shifts for cello, and notes and shifts encompassing half, first, second, and third positions on bass. Basic reading fluency in alto clef also should be expected.

Instrumental music education majors should add the following skills to the above list: scales using second, third, fourth, and fifth position on violin; scales using third position on viola, requiring a switch from alto to treble clef; scales from first through fourth positions on cello with a basic exploration of tenor clef and thumb position; and scales from half through fifth position on bass with a basic exploration of thumb position. Rudimentary vibrato should be demonstrated as well as the ability to finger and bow passages of intermediate difficulty on all four instruments. Exhibition of basic orchestra bowings should be expected.

All music education majors should demonstrate the following maintenance and repair skills: changing a string, lubricating a peg, removing or installing a fine tuner, straightening or setting up a bridge, adjusting or installing a chin rest, adjusting the length of an endpin or sharpening it, and properly tuning the instrument. In addition, all students should recognize the following adjustment problems: a tail gut that is too long or too short; pegs that do not fit; an incorrectly fitted bridge that is of improper height or warped; an open seam; an open crack; a fallen soundpost; a stripped bow screw; and buzzing due to a frayed string, incorrect bridge height, an open seam or crack, a loose fine tuner, or jewelry that a student is wearing.

The student should be familiar with accessories such as rosin, shoulder rests, and endpin protectors and should be conversant with terms such as "carved," "laminated," "fiberglass," "pernambuco," and other similar descriptors. Knowledge of proper chairs, cases, and storage racks also will be helpful.

Prospective string teachers need "hands-on" experiences early in their training. Some means of early exploration and direct contact with string students in the schools should exist even if there is no preparatory program. Furthermore, methods courses or techniques courses should be taught by teachers who have had recent, direct experiences with students in the elementary and secondary schools, and students should have access to such situations when taking these courses.

All instrumental majors (wind, percussion, and string players) should spend time in wind and string instructional situations and conduct both bands and orchestras at some level. Since student teaching can have a tremendous impact on a future teacher's orientation, values, and success, every effort should be made to place instrumental majors in balanced programs offering both band and orchestra activities. To do otherwise will perpetuate the cycle of a large pool of band-oriented teachers.

If the college sponsors any sort of string festival or orchestra activity for an area's young students, all music education majors in string methods classes should be involved. Methods students could assist with tuning, auditions, sectional rehearsals, and other aspects of the teaching, rehearsing, or administrative processes. The opportunity to play a string instrument either on a "rehearsals only" basis or as a performing member of such a group would be especially beneficial. Many nonstring majors have acquired strong secondary skills in this manner, and many have made a further commitment to school orchestra activities.

Prospective string teachers should possess sufficient keyboard skills to enable them to play simple accompaniments in their string classes. They also should have had a minimum of two semesters of conducting as well as the essential core courses such as theory, music history, sight singing, and ear training. All string students should be required to participate in ensemble experiences to provide them with extensive study in string literature, and this literature should include materials from solo, chamber, and orchestra works. These pieces should cover all historical periods from early music to contemporary styles and techniques.

Special classes should be designed or existing courses should include information regarding nonperformance activities such as scheduling, organizational techniques, budgets, and discipline. In addition, prospective string teachers need to become adept in dealing with administrators, parents, professional groups, and members of the music industry. They need to learn how to motivate students properly and use effective learning theories.

Cumulative field experiences should be included throughout a student's undergraduate studies. Students should begin with an observation period and lead up to actual teaching. While participating in field experiences, students should have structured, organized information on what to observe in the classroom and what the instructional objectives are, as well as activities that will lead toward a conceptual understanding in string performance. After a prescribed time they may assist in the instructional process under the direct supervision of a college professor and the supervising teacher. Because it is on a limited, exploratory basis, this is not to be construed as student teaching, but a part of the field experience.

The culmination of this preparation is student teaching. To be effective, time should be allocated in the schedule whereby student teachers are able to attend seminars on campus to discuss their experiences as they progress. The purpose of these seminars is to provide student teachers with a forum in which they may discuss problems or developments as they occur. Under no circumstances are they intended to usurp the supervising teacher's role; they should enhance understanding and clarify difficulties that may exist.

Postgraduation training

Training should not end with college graduation: Independent study should continue throughout the teaching career. Lessons, workshops, trade journals, and conventions all provide opportunities for growth. Teachers can take home an unused school string instrument over the weekend, holiday, or summer vacation for practice and experimentation. This will enable teachers to become better acquainted with many instruments over a period of several years. Occasionally during a string class a teacher can ask a student to conduct so he can play the student's part.

Teachers can seek advice from colleagues, teachers, or professional musicians. Questions can be asked informally while at rehearsal or at social gatherings. The area music dealer and repair person often are more than happy to share valuable information about strings and instruments with a music teacher.

Students who study privately are a valuable resource. They can be asked what their teachers suggest about certain problems. Many professional conductors depend upon their concertmasters and principal players for help.

Above all, one should not overlook the benefits derived from enrolling in graduate school courses, whether on an ad hoc basis or for a degree. Many classes are especially designed to assist teachers in meeting their immediate concerns. Some short-term summer courses lasting a week or weekend revolve around special topics for the string and orchestra teacher. Many school districts are committed to reimbursing tuition and other expenses relating to additional training.

PART II

GENERAL CARE OF INSTRUMENTS AND BOWS

1. Handle string instruments with care; they are delicate. Keep them in the case when not in use, and keep the latches closed. Do not drop or drag the instrument, even when it is in its case.
2. Return the instrument and bow to the case immediately after use, close the lid, and secure the latches.
3. Do not store the instrument in a hot place such as the trunk of a car.
4. Do not expose the case to direct sunlight.
5. Avoid sudden changes in temperature. If the instrument has been exposed to freezing temperatures for a prolonged time, leave it in the case and allow it to adjust slowly to room temperature. Sudden changes in temperature result in severe changes in humidity, causing the wood to expand or shrink. This may cause cracks in the wood or glue and permit joints to open. It also may cause warpage. The ideal humidity and temperature level for instrument storage is the same as that which is acceptable to the human body.
6. Keep the instrument and bow clean. Wipe loose rosin dust off the instrument, strings, and bow stick after every use, and clean the instrument regularly (see "Cleaning the instrument," page 21).
7. Do not release the string tension (see "Replacing strings," pages 21-22).
8. Have all cracks and openings repaired immediately.
9. Have both the instrument and bow inspected at least once a year by a professional string repair person (see "Annual checkup," page 22).
10. Loosen bow hair after playing and return the bow to the case. Turn bow screw counterclockwise to a point where all tension is released from the bow stick, but do not let the hair "hang." Leaving tension on the hair between use will damage the bow.
11. Hold the bow by the frog end; *do not touch the hair.*
12. Keep all polish, cleaner, cleaning cloths, or other sources of grease away from bow hair.
13. Do not allow people who have not had stringed instrument experience to handle the instrument or the bow.
14. Do not put music in a case under or on top of the instrument.
15. Carry spare strings, mutes, rosin, shoulder rest, and other loose parts in the accessory compartment of the case. If they do not fit into the accessory compartment with the lid closed, carry them separately.

Cleaning the instrument

It is good practice to clean the instrument on a monthly basis. First, check the instrument to be sure that there are no cracks or openings. If there are any cracks or open glue joints, *do not* wipe the instrument, touch the crack, or use any polish. Have it repaired by a reputable stringed instrument service first.

If there are no cracks or openings, take a soft cloth and wipe off all loose rosin dust. Then, using a facial tissue, apply a good violin cleaner polish that is designed to dissolve rosin dust but not harm the varnish. Rub a small area of the instrument until it is clean. Apply more cleaner to the tissue as needed, but do not pour cleaner on the instrument. When all foreign matter is dissolved, wipe the area dry with a clean tissue. Be sure that the instrument is wiped completely dry, since all residue of polish and dissolved rosin will catch more dirt.

The advantage of using tissue instead of cloth for cleaning stringed instruments is that one is more willing to use a new tissue than a new cloth for each usage. The more often the tissue is changed, the better the end result will be. A cloth saturated with polish and rosin simply moves the dirt around.

The fingerboard and bow stick also may be cleaned with violin cleaner. Be careful, however, not to get cleaner or polish on the hair or on the bowing area of the strings. Some areas are hard to clean, such as under the tailpiece, bridge, and chin rest and around the bridge. Cotton swabs are helpful for this function. These areas should be cleaned by a stringed instrument service at least once a year or whenever the instrument needs servicing. Never remove the strings and the bridge when cleaning the instrument. Remember, a clean instrument not only looks better but also sounds better. A layer of dirt on top of an instrument will impair its response and mute the sound.

Do not use harsh cleansers, furniture polish, or solvents on the instrument. While cleaning the instrument, check the strings. Frayed, worn, or wire-loose strings should be replaced.

Replacing strings

In general, the tension of the strings should not be released for any other reason than to replace them. Stringed instruments and their strings are constructed to withstand the full tension of the strings. Releasing string tension *does not* save strings but may result in additional wear on the strings and the instrument. It also may cause the bridge or soundpost to move. Pressure on top of the instrument is necessary to keep the soundpost properly lodged in place.

When it becomes necessary to change strings, do not remove or loosen all of the strings at once. Remove one string, replace it with the new string, and then bring the new string up to pitch. Follow the same procedure with the next string until all strings have been changed. Start by replacing the lowest string first, next go to the highest string, then the second lowest string, and finally the second highest string. This procedure ensures that the bridge and the soundpost will not move. Care should be taken that the bridge does not begin to lean toward the fingerboard. Should this happen, the bridge must be straightened. When doing this, it is helpful to loosen the strings slightly. When

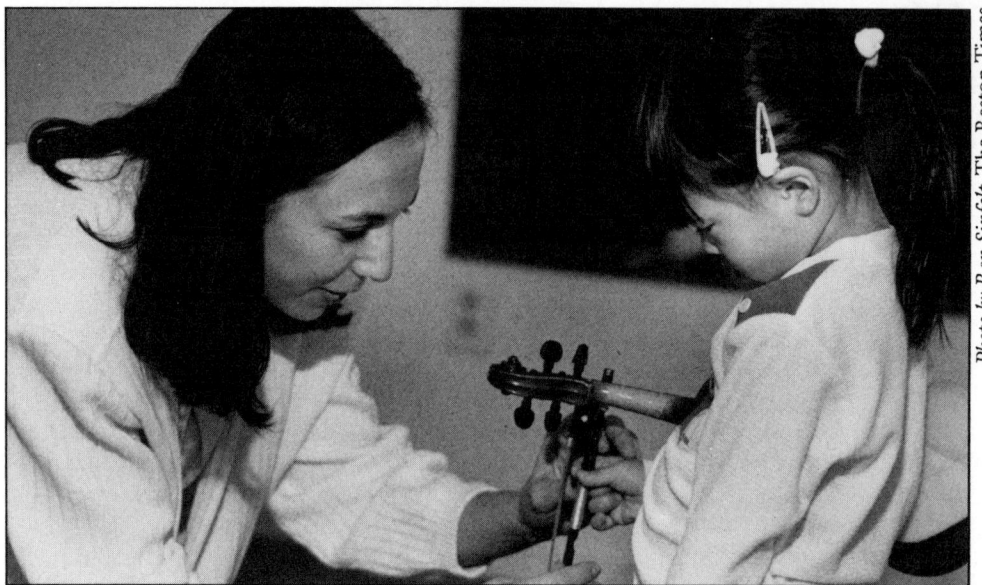

stringing an instrument, be sure that the strings are wound on the pegs in such a way that they do not crisscross. The laps of the string on the peg should roll toward the head side of the peg. This method helps to keep the peg in place and makes tuning easier.

Cracks and open glue joints

Any crack or open glue joint will impair the sound of the instrument, resulting in poor response or a rattle. Only persons trained and experienced in stringed instrument repair should attempt to fix these problems.

If an instrument has a crack or opening, do not wipe off rosin dust or use any kind of polish or cleaner. Do not touch or have anyone else touch the damaged area. Such actions can cause foreign matter to enter the crack, making the repair more difficult. Under no circumstance should you try to fix the crack with any type of household glue, white glue, or contact cement. It has been established that they are all inadequate and will only result in a higher repair cost. The cheapest and best way is to have a professional repair service do it right the first time. In addition, *never* have the bridge or soundpost glued to your instrument.

Annual checkup

Even if you believe there are no problems with the stringed instrument, it is good practice to take it at least once a year to a professional stringed instrument repair service for a complete checkup.

Separations and cracks

The instrument should be checked for hidden separations between top and ribs or back and ribs. The repair service also should check for any cracks and open joints that may have been overlooked.

Pegs
The pegs should be checked for proper fit and lubricated to ensure ease of turning with enough friction to hold the tension of the strings. Mechanical pegs also should be checked and adjusted for proper performance.

Fingerboard
The fingerboard should be inspected for wear and warpage. Any ripples or grooves will impair the sound and the playability of the instrument. Also check to see that the fingerboard is securely glued to the neck and blends in smoothly with the neck on both sides. The curvature should correspond with the curvature of the bridge. Use a straight edge to see that the length of the fingerboard is slightly concave.

String nut
The string nut should be checked to see that it is securely glued with the string grooves properly spaced and smooth to avoid damage to the strings. In addition, check to see that the strings clear the fingerboard but are not so high that they interfere with ease of fingering. A sharp edge on the first finger side of the nut should be filed down to avoid injury.

Bridge
The bridge should be checked to see that it is not warped, that the strings do not cut into the bridge, and that the string grooves are correctly spaced but not too deep. The bridge position on the violin should be checked and, if in the right place, it should be examined for its curvature and correct height (see page 29). A warped bridge should be replaced as soon as possible. A bridge jack is helpful in supporting strings while bridges are being replaced or repaired.

Soundpost
Check to see that the soundpost is in the right position, that it is not too long or too short, and that it fits well.

Tailpiece, tailgut, and string adjusters
The tailpiece should be examined to be certain that it is sized correctly. The tailgut should be the correct length. The adjusters should be snug, and the screws should work freely. There must be clearance between the top of the instrument and the bottom of the adjuster.

Chin rest
The chin rest should be checked to see if it is in the right position, if the clamp is securely tight, and if the cork or leather is glued to both plate and clamp. It should not be too tight to impair the sound or damage the instrument. There should be clearance between the chin rest and the tailpiece to prevent a rattling sound.

STRINGED INSTRUMENT AND EQUIPMENT CHECKLIST

OK   Needs Attention

Instrument:
_____ Cleaned _____ Polished _____   _____
_____ Pegs: Stick _____ Slip _____   _____
_____ Tension pegs: Loose _____ Need tightening _____   _____
_____ Strings: Wound straight on all pegs _____ Frayed _____
             False _____ Replace _____   _____
_____ Fingerboard: Clean _____ Grooved _____ Needs dressing _____   _____
_____ Bridge: Off-center _____ Leans _____ Warped _____
         Grooves too deep _____ Curvature too flat _____ Replace _____   _____
_____ Soundpost: In wrong place _____ Missing _____
_____ Tuners: Too low _____ Need to turn up _____
         Bent _____ Replace _____   _____
_____ Tail loop: Too long _____
_____ End button (violin and viola): Poor fit _____
_____ Endpin (cello and bass): Too short _____ Bent _____
_____ Opening in seams: Upper bout _____ Lower bout _____ Sides _____   _____
_____ Open cracks: In top _____ At bottom saddle _____
         In rib _____ Other _____   _____

Bow:
_____ Tightened too tightly _____
_____ Bow grip: Loose _____ Missing _____ Needs replacement _____   _____
_____ Bow stick: Needs cleaning _____ Warped _____ Too straight _____   _____
_____ Bow facing: Cracked _____ Chipped _____
         Missing tip _____ Replace _____   _____
_____ Frog: Cracked _____ Ferrule loose _____
         Slide cracked _____ Screw worn _____   _____
_____ Bow Hair: Twisted _____ Dirty _____ Needs rosin _____
         Rehair _____ Replace _____   _____

Case:
_____ Fasteners: Loose _____ Lock doesn't close tightly _____
_____ Handles: Worn _____ Loose _____ Replace _____
_____ Bow Clips: Bent _____ Worn _____ Broken _____
_____ Recommend instrument be covered in case _____   _____

Miscellaneous:
_____ Shoulder pad _____   _____
_____ Endpin stop (cellos and basses) _____   _____
_____ Cleaning cloth _____   _____

The following book is needed: _____

Other problems: _____

Instrument #: _____   Name of student: _____
Date work completed: _____   Teacher's signature: _____

PART III

CONSTRUCTION FEATURES OF INSTRUMENTS

Almost all stringed instruments are made of maple and spruce. Differences in quality are the result of the choice of materials, the construction method, and the quality of workmanship applied in the making of an instrument.

Basic maple and spruce student violins may have a pressed top and back, since pressing is the least time-consuming manufacturing method. Purfling (a decorated border) is often painted, not inlaid. If well adjusted, such instruments are acceptable for beginners only.

Other student instruments have carved tops and backs sculpted from a board 3/4" thick. This method, although more time consuming, usually results in better sounding instruments. These instruments also are usually equipped with a genuine inlaid purfling, which gives additional protection against cracking. If well adjusted, these make highly recommended student instruments.

Better grade or "step-up" instruments should be made of at least five-year-old loft-seasoned tops and backs and should always be carved and graduated. They also should be purfled and adjusted for best tonal results and easy playing.

Pegs

Pegs are of two major types: friction pegs and tension pegs.

Friction pegs are the traditional pegs that have been used for centuries on all kinds of musical instruments and rely on the friction between the peg box of the scroll and the peg itself to stay tight. Proper and precise fitting is essential. The taper of the peg and the taper of the hole in the peg box have to be a perfect match, and both the hole and the peg have to be perfectly round. Special tools are needed to achieve the perfect fit. Peg compound should be applied to the contact areas for smooth turning and secure holding of the pegs. There are compounds that will accommodate both needs. Since most stringed instruments are made abroad and shipped, some time should be allowed for the wood to settle and adjust to the climate in the United States before doing any work on them. When constructed abroad, the hole in the peg box as well as the peg frequently "get out of round" (become egg shaped) and should be drilled or reshaped here.

When peg holes are drilled, care should be taken in alignment so the strings wound on the upper pegs do not touch the lower pegs. Enough clearance between the back of the peg box and the pegs is important so that strings wind freely on the peg and do not rub against the back. Poorly fitted pegs can result in peg box cracks, which necessitate difficult repairs. If friction pegs are selected, insist on a good-quality ebony peg. Ebonized pegs, hardwood pegs, or plastic pegs do not provide satisfactory results and should be avoided. Some better instruments are fitted with rosewood or boxwood pegs, which are decorative and usually costly. They do not function any better, however, than a well-fitted ebony peg.

Tension pegs (those with mechanical features like screws) were invented to make tuning easier. Extreme care should be taken, however, when choosing tension pegs. Few tension pegs really do what they were intended to do. A good tension peg should enable students to be able to learn to tune their instruments sooner. The peg should not stick in high humidity or slip in low humidity. Tension pegs should also be maintenance free. Only the best tension pegs really give you these features. Poorly designed tension pegs will usually fail. Beware of tension pegs that "expand."

Fingerboard

The fingerboard should be made of ebony. Some ebony used on less expensive instruments may be striped (black-brown), which is acceptable. So-called "ebonized fingerboards" are stained hardwood and are too soft. They wear out quickly and lose their shape. The shape of the fingerboard and neck is of great importance since it affects the playing of the instrument. The fingerboard should be fitted to the neck so that there are no edges or ridges. The curve of the fingerboard should be such that it matches the curve of the bridge. In its entire length, the fingerboard should be slightly concave, free of ripples, warpage, or twisting.

On violas and cellos, fingerboards are made with or without the "C" bevel. Both shapes are acceptable, and the choice is a matter of personal preference.

The distance from the end of the fingerboard to the top of the instrument should be as follows:

	Minimum		Maximum
4/4 violin	19.0mm	–	21mm
4/4 viola	23.0mm	–	25mm
4/4 cello	62.0mm	–	65mm
Standard bass	9.5cm	–	11cm

The fingerboard should be aligned with the neck and with the center line of the instrument.

String nut

The string nut at the upper end of the fingerboard should be made of ebony. On the violin and viola, it should be shaped so that the strings are slightly above the fingerboard (about the thickness of a business card). The space will be proportionally higher for the cello and bass. The string grooves should be just deep enough to hold the strings in place (about one-third the diameter of the string) and should be smooth so that they do not pinch or bind the string.

The approximate spacing of the strings from center to center should be:

4/4 violin	6.0mm
4/4 viola	6.5mm
4/4 cello	8.0mm
Standard bass	10.0mm

Bridge

The bridge should be carved out of quartered maple and should be fitted to the instrument. Adjustable bridges with movable feet are acceptable *if fitted and adjusted* as a carved bridge. The feet should be fitted properly to the belly of the instrument, and the curvature of the bridge should be adjusted to match the fingerboard so that the strings have proper clearance. The string grooves should be spaced properly, be smooth, and be just deep enough to hold strings in place (one-half the diameter of the string). The side of the bridge facing the fingerboard should be slightly rounded (have a belly). All bridges should be thinned at the top to match the thickness of the heaviest string. The feet should be fitted in a way that the back of the bridge (facing the tailpiece) forms a 90-degree angle with the top of the instrument. On student instruments, bridges with a rounder curvature are preferable, since this makes it easier to bow one string at a time. The spacing of the strings (from center to center) should be:

4/4 violin	12mm
4/4 viola	13mm
4/4 cello	16mm
Standard bass	25mm

BRIDGE CURVATURES AND STRING HEIGHTS

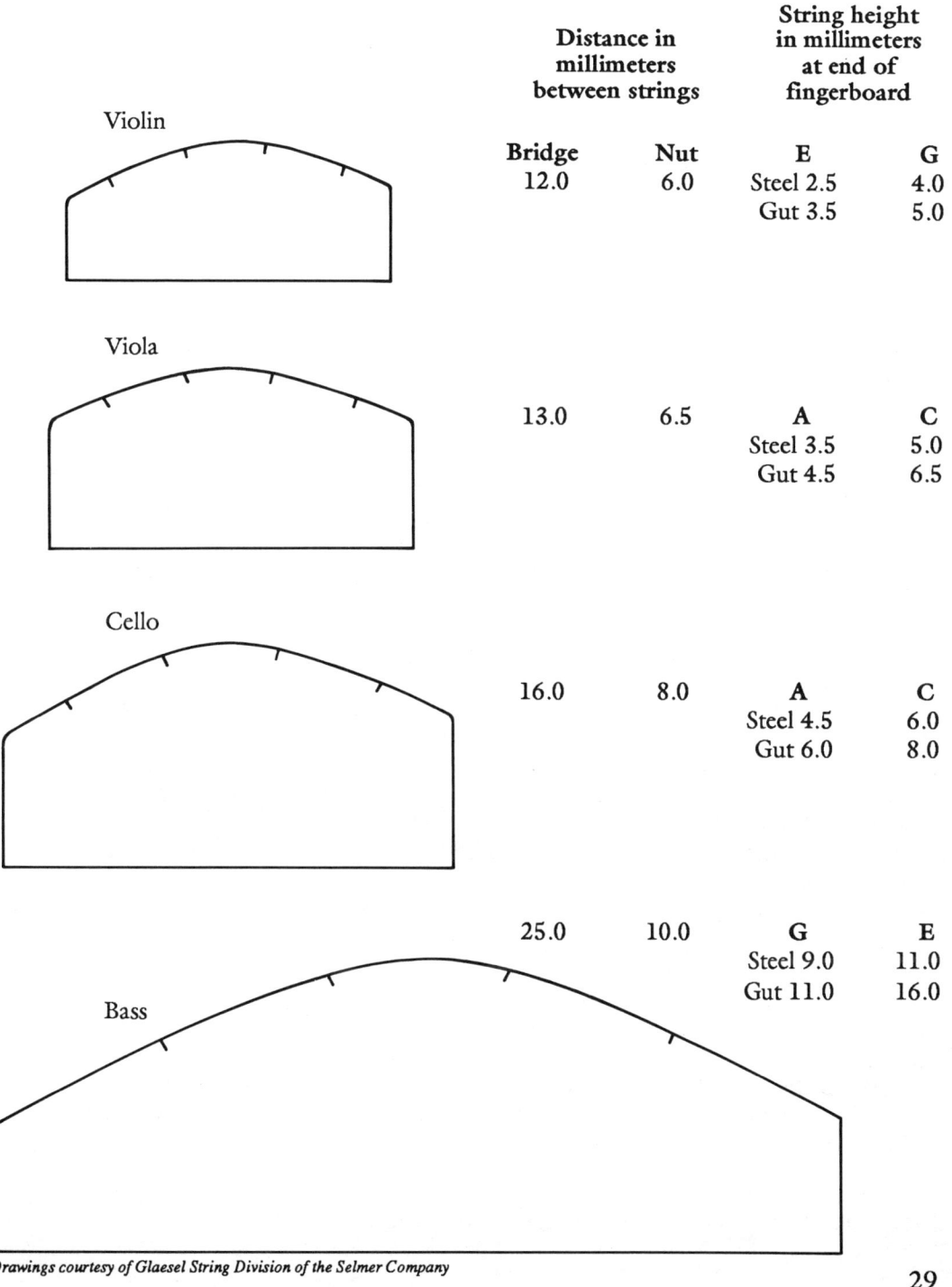

	Distance in millimeters between strings		String height in millimeters at end of fingerboard	
	Bridge	**Nut**		
Violin	12.0	6.0	**E** Steel 2.5 Gut 3.5	**G** 4.0 5.0
Viola	13.0	6.5	**A** Steel 3.5 Gut 4.5	**C** 5.0 6.5
Cello	16.0	8.0	**A** Steel 4.5 Gut 6.0	**C** 6.0 8.0
Bass	25.0	10.0	**G** Steel 9.0 Gut 11.0	**E** 11.0 16.0

Drawings courtesy of Glaesel String Division of the Selmer Company

String height above the end of the fingerboard should be:*

Instrument	String	Steel strings	Wound-on-gut and perlon strings
4/4 violin	E	2.5mm	
	G		4.0mm
	E		3.5mm
	G		5.0mm
4/4 viola	A	3.5mm	
	C		5.0mm
	A		4.5mm
	C		6.5mm
4/4 cello	A	4.5mm	
	C		6.0mm
	A		6.0mm
	C		8.0mm
Standard bass	G	9.0mm	
	E		11.0mm
	G		11.0mm
	E		16.0mm

Bridges with adjustable feet are acceptable on all instruments, providing the height of the bridge is adjusted to give the right string height at the end of the fingerboard. Since humidity changes can influence the string height on basses, they should be equipped with bridges with height adjustment wheels for ease of playing.

Soundpost

The soundpost should be a round piece of even-grained, quartered spruce. It should be of the correct size for the instrument and should fit snugly against the top and back. The soundpost position and length greatly influence the sound of the instrument. Because it may need to be adjusted or changed, the soundpost should *never* be glued down. The soundpost position is behind the bridge foot under the highest string of the instrument (see figure 1). The diameters for the soundpost are:

4/4 violin	6.25mm
4/4 viola	7.00mm
4/4 cello	11.00mm
Standard bass	19.00 to 21.00mm

Saddle

The saddle should be made of ebony. It should be fitted into the top, and it must be high enough so that it will not touch the top when the tailpiece is fitted properly.

---

*The height should be lower for steel strings than for wound-on-gut or perlon strings.

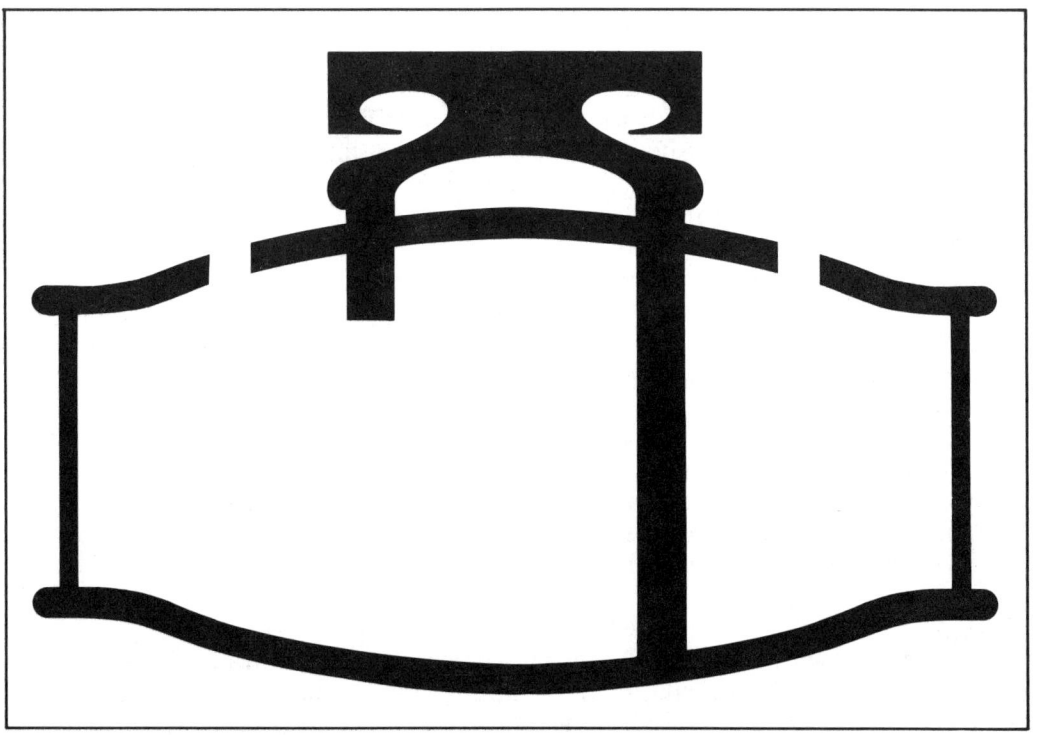

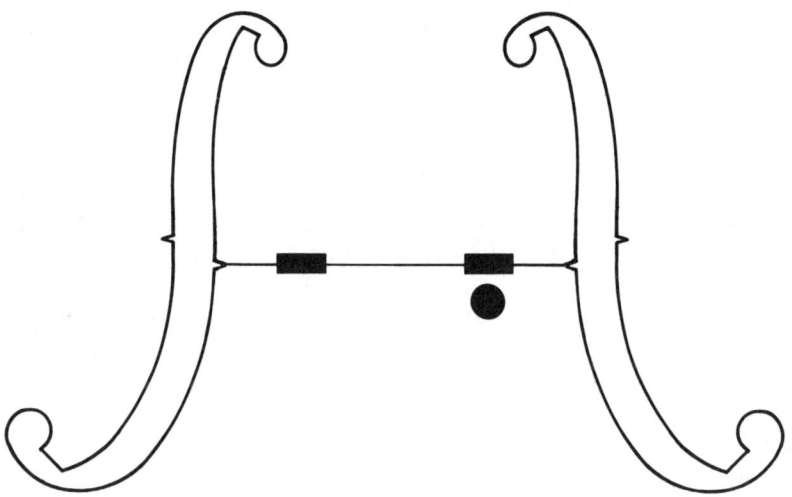

Note: The proper position of the bridge on the instrument is for the bridge to be evenly spaced between the F-holes and the F-notches pointing to the center of the bridge feet.

Figure 1.

Drawings courtesy of Glaesel String Division of the Selmer Company

Tailpiece and the tailpiece hanger

The tailpiece should be of ebony. Hardwood or plastic tailpieces are unacceptable. Good-quality metal tailpieces with built-in adjusters are acceptable for instruments equipped with four steel strings. If four steel strings are used with ebony tailpieces, they should be fitted with four individual fine tuners.

The tailhanger should be made of nylon or perlon with threaded ends and brass nuts for easy fitting and adjusting.

Bass tailhangers should be made of brass wire one-eighth inch in diameter, threaded on both ends, and secured with capnuts.

Note: On basses, hardwood tailpieces are acceptable in order to save weight.

The tailhanger should be fitted so that the tailpiece, even under full string tension, almost touches the saddle.

Endpin

The endpin should be made of ebony or metal. It is about eighteen inches long on standard cellos and about fifteen inches long on small-size cellos. On a standard bass, the endpin is usually fifteen inches to eighteen inches. Shorter endpins on either instruments should not be accepted.

Strings

The strings should be of good quality, precision made, and matched. Bare metal, metal-wound-on-metal, metal-wound-on-gut, metal-wound-on-perlon, or nylon strings are being used. Metal and metal-wound-on-metal strings are usually more brilliant sounding than strings of wound-on gut or perlon, which usually have a mellower sound.

It is advisable to start beginning students on instruments equipped with chromium steel strings and four fine tuners on the tailpiece. Steel strings are not influenced by humidity and require less retuning. Quite often the tuning of the instrument is done by the teacher at the beginning of the lesson, and if the student uses anything other than a chromium steel string, he will probably practice between lessons on an out-of-tune instrument. After the student has learned to tune his own instrument, it may be advisable to switch to metal-wound-on-gut or metal-wound-on-perlon strings.

Chromium steel strings are available for violin, viola, cello, and bass and are usually supplied in fractional sizes for smaller instruments. The violin E string is usually a solid steel wire; all other steel strings are usually wound with a flat chromium steel band. Some brands also offer steel strings in three gauges such as soft, medium, and hard. Medium strings should be used on student instruments. String gauges for violin, viola, and cello are listed in table 1.

Chin rests

Chin rests are available in ebony, rosewood, boxwood, and various plastic materials. Student violins are usually equipped with plastic chin rests to make them less expensive. A chin rest should be comfortable and free of sharp edges and ridges. Cork or leather must be attached to both the clamp and plate at the points of contact with the instrument.

Adjusters

Adjusters or fine tuners should be used with all steel strings. Tailpieces with built-in adjusters are available for young students. Wound-on-gut and wound-on-perlon strings should not have fine tuners because of the limited tuning range with these strings. Since string basses come equipped with brass machine heads, fine tuners are not needed.

Table 1

Wound-on-gut strings are available in a wide variety of gauges. The following is a list of medium string gauges. The gauges are given in three standard measurements. PM(Pirastro Measure™) is an internationally accepted gauging system for strings.

Instrument	String	PM*	Diameter (mm)	Inch	Materials used
Violin	E	5.25	0.26	.0104	chrome steel, goldplated steel, aluminum wound on steel
	A	13.50	0.675	.027	aluminum wound on gut, aluminum wound on perlon
	D	17.00	0.85	.034	aluminum wound on gut, aluminum wound on perlon
	G	16.00	0.80	.032	silver wound on gut, silver wound on perlon
Viola	A	14.00	0.70	.028	aluminum wound on gut, aluminum wound on perlon
	D	17.00	0.85	.034	aluminum wound on gut, aluminum wound on perlon
	G	16.00	0.80	.032	silver wound on gut, silver wound on perlon
	C	21.50	1.08	.043	silver wound on gut, silver wound on perlon
Cello	A	20.00	1.00	.040	aluminum wound on gut, aluminum wound on perlon
	D	27.00	1.35	.054	aluminum wound on gut, aluminum wound on perlon
	G	26.00	1.30	.052	silver wound on gut, silverplated copper wound on gut, silver wound on perlon, flat chrome wound on perlon
	C	36.00	1.80	.072	silver wound on gut, silverplated copper wound on gut, silver wound on perlon, chrome wound on perlon

*1 PM = .05mm = .002"

Shoulder pads

Shoulder pads can increase a player's comfort and technical facility. There are many types of pads available, and one should be selected to accommodate the physical characteristics of the student. Not all students, however, require a shoulder pad, nor do all teachers recommend their use.

Bows

Bows are available in a wide range of choices. The basic three types of materials used in bows are fiberglass, brazilwood, and pernambuco.

Pernambuco bows are available in a wide price range. Pernambuco wood is the most desirable material in bow sticks. Pernambuco bows, suitable for the advanced student, are equipped with ebony frogs with nickel silver trim and unbleached horsehair. Higher grade pernambuco bows may have silver and gold trim and cost as much as several thousand dollars.

Fiberglass bows are manufactured in all sizes for all instruments and are available with synthetic hair, genuine horsehair, plastic grips, and wire grips. They keep their shape better than do most inexpensive wood bows. Because of their outstanding durability under rugged school conditions and low cost, fiberglass bows are suggested for the beginning student. Synthetic hair may also be used with beginners because of its durability and low cost, but it does not wear as well as horsehair.

Brazilwood bows are considered student bows. Usually brazilwood bows come equipped with ebony frogs, nickel silver trim, and horsehair. They are acceptable for beginning students; however, because of the nature of the material, these bows lose their shape easily if left in the case with tightened hair. (In fact, this applies to all wooden bows.)

Cherry and beech bows may be of extremely poor quality and are not acceptable for student use.

Cases

Cases should be of proper size and made out of either vacuum-molded thermoplastic material with aluminum extrusion or laminated (plywood) veneer with keratol covering and weatherstripping or screw-attached cordura covering with three heavy-duty hinges, two drawback latches, and a sturdy, molded handle riveted to aluminum extrusion.* Thermoplastic cases should be reinforced with polyurethane foam. All cases should be plush lined.

All cases should be made to fit the size of the instrument and bow in order to give maximum protection. Instrument cases should be able to withstand at least 150 pounds of pressure. Cello cases are also available in polyshell and thermoplastic construction.

---

*Applies only to vacuum-molded cases.

PART IV

Photo by Robin Layton

WRITING SPECIFICATIONS

Be precise in the requirements you set in your specifications. Vague terms will result in poor-quality instruments being offered, which will endanger the success of your program. Poorly constructed and adjusted instruments make it impossible for your students to perform and are a major cause for failure.

Writing specifications

In writing bid specifications, it is always advisable to use the manufacturer's model number for the product you wish to purchase. Consult manufacturer's catalogs whenever possible to ensure that the equipment ordered meets your expectations. Do not accept equipment that does not conform to specifications. Examine it to be certain that it is acceptable. If it is not, return it for replacement. (See also "Concepts in purchasing," page 45.)

Specifications for violin and viola outfits*
Basic-quality student violin outfit:

Carved, pressed, or maple back, flamed scroll, back, and sides. Material loft seasoned. Carved spruce top of quartered, fine-grained spruce, fully graduated, loft seasoned. Fitted bass bar of spruce, genuine or painted purfling† around top and back. The ribs to be bent of solid maple with four solid corner blocks and upper and lower blocks. Full lining around top and back. Lining, end, and corner blocks of spruce or willow.

Ebony pegs, well seasoned, trued and fitted in the United States, or highest quality, precision-made rosewood tension pegs fitted in the United States.

Bridge of hard maple, fitted in the United States.

Soundpost of medium fine-grained spruce of correct diameter and size, fitted in the United States.

Fingerboard and string nut of ebony, serviced and adjusted in the United States.

Tailpiece of ebony, equipped with nylon tailhanger, threaded on both ends with nonslipping brass nuts, properly adjusted. Four individual fine tuners securely attached (or metal tailpiece of proper size with four built-in fine tuners*) with nylon tailhanger, threaded on both ends with nonslip brass nuts and properly adjusted.

Four chromium steel strings of good quality, medium gauge, and proper length and diameter.

---

*Recommendations for minimum specifications for basic-quality student viola outfits are the same as for violins.
†State only one choice to avoid receiving unacceptable equipment.

Inside label to carry the manufacturer's name and model number, size, serial number, and date of adjustment in the United States.

Bow: Fiberglass or brazilwood bow* of correct size and weight with firmly attached wire or plastic* grip (soldered on both ends†), firmly secured thumb leather, and synthetically bleached or natural, unbleached, genuine horsehair.*

Case: Case of proper size and made from vacuum-molded thermoplastic materials with aluminum extrusion or laminated (plywood) veneer with keratol covering and weatherstripping or screw-attached cordura covering,* with three heavy-duty hinges, two drawback latches, and a sturdy, molded handle riveted to the aluminum extrusion.‡ Thermoplastic case to be reinforced with polyurethane foam. All cases to be plush lined.

Rosin: Request good quality in a plastic or wooden holder with a cardboard cover.

Intermediate-quality student violin outfit:§

Violin to be constructed of carved, well-flamed maple scroll and back, solid maple sides. Material properly loft seasoned. Carved spruce top made of quartered, fine-grained spruce, fully graduated and properly seasoned. Fitted bass bar of spruce, with genuine purfling around top and back.

Ebony pegs, well seasoned, trued, and fitted in the United States, or highest quality, precision-made rosewood tension pegs fitted in the United States.

Bridge of good, hard maple, fitted in the United States. Soundpost of medium fine-grained spruce of correct diameter and size, fitted in the United States.

Fingerboard and string nut of ebony, serviced and adjusted in the United States.

Tailpiece of ebony, equipped with nylon tailhanger, threaded on both ends with nonslipping brass nuts, properly adjusted. Two individual fine tuners securely attached.

Chromium steel E and A strings, aluminum-on-gut D string, and silver-on-gut G string of good quality.

Inside label to carry the manufacturer's name and model number, size, serial number, and date of adjustment in the United States.

Bow: Brazilwood bow with ebony frog and nickel silver trim of correct size and weight, with firmly attached wire or plastic* grip (soldered on both ends†), firmly secured thumb leather and natural, unbleached, genuine horsehair.

Case: Case of proper size and made from vacuum-molded thermoplastic materials with aluminum extrusion or laminated (plywood) veneer with keratol covering and weatherstripping or screwed-attached cordura covering,* with three heavy-duty hinges, two drawback latches, and a sturdy, molded handle riveted to the aluminum extrusion.‡ Thermoplastic case to be reinforced with polyurethane foam. All cases to be plush lined.

---

*State only one choice to avoid receiving unacceptable equipment.
†Applies only to wire grip.
‡Applies only to vacuum-molded cases.
§Recommendations for minimum specifications for intermediate-quality student viola outfits are the same as for violins.

Rosin: Request good quality rosin in a plastic or wood holder with a cardboard cover.

Advanced-quality student violin outfit:

Violin to be constructed of carved, flamed maple scroll and back, solid maple sides. Material properly loft seasoned. Carved spruce top made of European, quartered, fine-grained spruce, fully graduated and properly loft seasoned. Fitted bass bar of spruce, with genuine purfling around top and back.

Ebony pegs, well-seasoned, trued and fitted in the United States, or highest quality precision-made rosewood tension pegs, fitted in the United States.

Bridge of select-quality maple, fitted in the United States.

Soundpost of medium fine-grained spruce of correct diameter and size, fitted in the United States.

Fingerboard and string nut of fine-quality ebony, serviced and adjusted in the United States.

Tailpiece of ebony, equipped with nylon tailhanger, threaded on both ends with nonslipping brass nuts, properly adjusted. Fine tuners securely attached.

Steel E string, aluminum-wound-on-gut or perlon A and D strings, silver-wound-on-gut or perlon G string of good quality, medium gauge, and proper diameter.

Inside label to carry the manufacturer's name and model number, size, serial number, and date of adjustment in United States.

Bow: Pernambuco wood bow with ebony frog, nickel silver or silver* trim, of correct size and weight, with firmly attached wire or whalebone* grip (soldered on both ends†) firmly secured thumb leather, and natural, unbleached, genuine horsehair.

Case: Oblong case of proper size made from black, vacuum-molded thermoplastic materials with aluminum extrusion or laminated veneer with keratol or canvas covering and weatherstripping,* with three heavy-duty hinges, two drawback latches, and a sturdy, molded handle riveted to aluminum extrusion.‡ Case to be reinforced with polyurethane foam. Case to be plush lined.

Rosin: Request good-quality, professional-type rosin in cloth container.

Specifications for cello outfits
Basic-quality cello outfit:

Cello to be constructed of laminated maple back and sides, laminated spruce top, and carved maple neck and scroll. Top to have a fitted bass bar made of seasoned spruce. Tops and back not purfled. Ribs of laminated maple with four solid corner blocks, upper and lower blocks, full lining around top and back. Blocks and lining of spruce or willow.

Pegs of well-seasoned ebony, trued and fitted in the United States, or highest quality precision-made rosewood tension pegs, fitted in the United States.

---

*State only one choice to avoid receiving unacceptable equipment.
†Applies only to wire grip.
‡Applies only to vacuum-molded cases.

Bridge of good-quality hard maple, fitted in the United States.

Soundpost of medium fine-grained spruce of correct diameter and size, fitted in the United States.

Fingerboard and string nut of good-quality seasoned ebony, fitted, serviced, and adjusted in the United States.

Tailpiece of ebony with four fine tuners (or metal* with four built-in fine tuners) with nylon tailhanger, threaded on both ends with nonslip brass nuts and properly adjusted. Endpin to be properly fitted with hardwood or ebony socket, heavy-duty, eighteen-inch endpin and set screw.

Four chromium steel strings of good quality, medium gauge, and of proper length and diameter.

Inside label to carry manufacturer's name and model number, size, serial number, and date of adjustment in the United States.

Bow: Brazilwood or fiberglass* bow of correct size and weight with firmly attached wire or plastic* grip (soldered on both ends†), firmly secured thumb leather, synthetic or natural, unbleached, genuine horsehair.

Cover: Soft plastic or canvas* material, fleece-lined to protect instrument. To be equipped with a zipper closure to open on one side at least up to the neckjoint of the instrument, a sturdy handle, and at least one bow pocket, one string pocket, and one music pocket. Cover to be of proper size for instrument.

Outfit to be supplied with a large cake of good-quality rosin in a plastic or wood container with a cardboard cover and an endpin rest.

Intermediate-quality student cello outfit:

Back, scroll, and neck to be carved from solid, flamed maple. Material loft seasoned. Top to be carved from solid, quartered spruce, seasoned, graduated, and fitted with a bass bar, made of a separate piece of spruce. Sides to be bent from solid maple, matching scroll and back, fitted with four solid corner blocks, upper and lower block, and full lining around top and back. Blocks and lining to be of spruce or willow.

Pegs of well-seasoned ebony, trued and fitted in the United States, or highest quality, precision-made rosewood tension pegs, fitted in the United States.

Soundpost of medium-fine, straight-grained spruce of correct diameter and size, fitted in the United States.

Fingerboard and string nut to be of good-quality, seasoned ebony and fitted, serviced, and adjusted in the United States.

Tailpiece of ebony with two fine tuners and nylon tailhanger, threaded on both ends with nonslip brass nuts and properly adjusted in the United States.

Endpin to be fitted with hardwood or ebony socket, with a heavy-duty eighteen-inch endpin and set screw.

Chromium A and D strings of good quality and silver or silverplated wire-wound-on-gut or perlon G and C strings of proper length and diameter.

Inside label to carry manufacturer's name, model number, size, serial number, and date of adjustment in the United States.

---

*State only one choice to avoid receiving unacceptable equipment.
†Applies only to wire grip.

Bow: Brazilwood or fiberglass bow* with firmly attached wire or plastic* grip (soldered on both ends†), firmly secured thumb leather, and natural, unbleached, genuine horsehair.

Cover: Waterproof canvas or cordura, lined with fleece or tricot, with a foam padding between inner and outer layer. To be equipped with zipper fastener, a sturdy handle, and at least one bow pocket, one string pocket, and a music pocket.

Outfit to be supplied with an endpin rest and a large piece of good-quality rosin in plastic or wood container with cardboard cover.

Advanced-quality student cello outfit:

Back, scroll, and neck to be carved from solid, well-flamed maple. Material properly loft seasoned. Top to be carved from straight-grained, solid, quartered spruce and properly seasoned, graduated, and fitted with a bass bar from a separate piece of spruce. Sides to be bent from solid maple matching scroll and back, fitted with four solid corner blocks, upper and lower block and full lining around top and back. Blocks and lining of spruce or willow.

Pegs of well-seasoned ebony, trued and fitted in the United States, or highest quality, precision-made rosewood tension pegs, fitted in the United States.

Bridge of good-quality hard maple, fitted in the United States.

Soundpost of medium-fine, straight-grained spruce and of correct diameter and size, fitted in the United States.

Fingerboard and string nut of select, seasoned ebony, fitted, serviced, and adjusted in the United States.

Tailpiece of ebony with one fine tuner and with nylon tailhanger, threaded on both ends with nonslip brass nuts and properly adjusted in the United States.

Endpin to be fitted with hardwood socket, with a heavy-duty eighteen-inch endpin and set screw.

Chromium A string of fine quality, aluminum-wound-on-gut or perlon D string of good quality, and silver-wire-wound-on-gut or perlon G and C strings of proper length and diameter.

Inside label to carry manufacturer's name, model number, size, serial number, and date of adjustment in the United States.

Bow: Pernambuco wood with ebony frog, nickel silver or silver* trimmed, with firmly attached wire or whalebone* grip (soldered on both ends†), firmly secured thumb leather, and genuine, natural, unbleached, white horsehair.

Cover: Waterproof cordura or nylon with tricot lining, with foam padding between the inner and outer layers. To be equipped with zipper fastener, a sturdy handle, and at least one bow pocket, one string pocket, and a music pocket.

Outfit to be supplied with an endpin rest and a large cake of good-quality rosin in a plastic or wood container with a cardboard cover.

---

*State only one choice to avoid receiving unacceptable equipment.
†Applies only to wire grip.

Specifications for bass outfits:

Basic-quality student bass outfit:

Bass made of laminated (plywood) veneer, maple back and sides, with laminated top and solid, carved neck and scroll. Top to have a fitted bass bar made of seasoned spruce. Top and back to have genuine or painted purfling.* Ribs of laminated maple with four solid corner blocks and upper and lower blocks. Fully lined around top and back and with full carnis. Blocks and lining of spruce or willow.

Bass to be equipped with solid brass machine heads, preferably nickel plated, Tyrolean style.

Bridge of good quality, fitted in the United States, and equipped with height adjustment mechanism. Soundpost of medium-fine spruce of correct diameter and size, fitted in the United States.

Fingerboard and string nut of good-quality, seasoned ebony and fitted, serviced, and adjusted in the United States.

Tailpiece of ebonized hardwood with one-eighth-inch solid brass, annealed wire hanger, threaded on both ends, and equipped with cap nuts.

Endpin to be properly fitted. Rosewood or ebony socket with eighteen-inch heavy-duty rod and set screw.

Good-quality chromium steel strings of medium gauge and proper length and diameter.

Bow: Fiberglass or brazilwood* bow, French model (or if preferred, German model*) of proper size and weight with firmly attached wire or plastic* grip (soldered on both ends†), firmly secured thumb leather, and synthetically bleached or natural, unbleached, genuine horsehair.

Cover: Soft plastic or canvas* material, fleece-lined to protect instrument. To be equipped with a zipper closure to open on one side at least up to neck-joint of the instrument, a sturdy handle, and at least one bow pocket, one string pocket, and one music pocket. Cover to be of proper size for instrument.

Outfit to be supplied with a large cake of medium-grade bass rosin (poured into a metal container in a cardboard or plastic box) and an endpin rest.

Intermediate-quality student bass outfit:

Bass made of laminated, flamed maple back and sides, with solid spruce, carved top, and solid, carved neck and scroll. Top to have a fitted bass bar made of seasoned spruce. Top to be purfled. Ribs of laminated maple with four solid corner blocks and upper and lower blocks, fully lined around top and back and with full carnis. Blocks and lining of spruce or willow.

Bass to be equipped with solid brass machine heads, preferably nickel plated, Tyrolean style.

Bridge of good quality, fitted in the United States, and equipped with height adjustment mechanism.

Soundpost of medium fine-grained spruce of correct diameter and size, fit-

---

*State only one choice to avoid receiving unacceptable equipment.
†Applies only to wire grip.

ted in the United States.

Fingerboard and string nut of good-quality, seasoned ebony, fitted, serviced, and adjusted in the United States.

Tailpiece of ebonized hardwood or ebony with one-eighth-inch solid brass, annealed wire hanger, threaded on both ends, and equipped with cap nuts.

Endpin to be properly fitted. Rosewood or ebony socket with eighteen-inch heavy-duty rod and set screw.

Good-quality chromium steel strings of medium gauge and of proper length and diameter.

Bow: Brazilwood bow with ebony frog and nickel silver ring, French or German* model of proper size and weight with firmly attached wire or plastic* grip (soldered on both ends†), firmly secured thumb leather, and natural, unbleached, genuine horsehair.

Case: Cordura or canvas material, lined to protect instrument. To be equipped with zipper fasteners to open on one side at least up to neckjoint of the instrument, a sturdy handle, and at least one bow pocket, one string pocket, and one music pocket. Cover to be of proper size for instrument.

Outfit supplied with a large cake of medium-grade bass rosin (poured into a metal container in cardboard or plastic box) and an endpin rest.

Advanced-quality student bass:

Bass carved of seasoned, solid, flamed maple back and sides with solid, carved spruce top and solid, carved neck and scroll. Top to have a fitted bass bar made of loft-seasoned spruce. Top and back to be purfled. Tops and backs properly loft seasoned. Ribs of solid, flamed maple with four solid corner blocks and upper and lower blocks, fully lined around top and back and with full carnis. Blocks and lining of spruce or willow.

Bass equipped with solid brass machine heads, preferably nickel plated, Tyrolean style.

Bridge of select-quality maple, fitted in the United States, and equipped with height adjustment mechanism.

Soundpost of medium, fine-grained spruce, of correct diameter and size, fitted in the United States.

Fingerboard and string nut of good quality, seasoned ebony, fitted, serviced, and adjusted in the United States.

Tailpiece of ebonized hardwood or ebony with one-eighth-inch solid brass, annealed wire to cable hanger, threaded on both ends, and equipped with cap nuts.

Endpin to be properly fitted. Rosewood or ebony socket with eighteen-inch heavy-duty rod and set screw.

Good-quality chromium steel strings of medium gauge and of proper length and diameter.

Bow: Pernambuco wood bow with ebony frog and nickel silver ring, French or German* model of proper size and weight with firmly attached wire

---

*State only one choice to avoid receiving unacceptable equipment.
†Applies only to wire grip.

or whalebone* grip (soldered on both ends†), firmly secured thumb leather, and natural, unbleached, genuine horsehair.

Cover: Waterproof cordura material, lined and padded to protect the instrument. (Any other material of equal strength and durability is acceptable.) The case should have a heavy-duty zipper closure to open on one side at least up to neckjoint of the instrument, a sturdy handle, and at least one bow pocket, one string pocket, and one music pocket. Cover to be of proper size for instrument.

Outfit to be supplied with a large cake of medium-grade bass rosin (poured into a metal container in a cardboard or plastic box) and an endpin rest.

---

*State only one choice to avoid receiving unacceptable equipment.
†Applies only to wire grip.

CHECKING YOUR PURCHASE

The body of the instrument

To be certain that your purchase complies with the specifications (see pages 36-43), there are a number of items that should be checked.

1. Be certain that the woods in the body of the instrument and the bow comply with your order. (For example, if you have specified spruce or maple, do not accept plywood.)
2. Check the alignment on the neck and fingerboard in relation to the body of the instrument to be certain that it has been shop adjusted in this country.
3. Check the pegs to see that they conform to the specifications.
4. Be sure that the tailpiece loop is just long enough so that the end of the tailpiece is even with the center of the saddle, extending slightly over the peak of the tailpiece.
5. Be certain that the metal tuner does not extend above the top of the tailpiece so far that it depresses the tailpiece. Also make sure that it does not extend below the tailpiece far enough to scratch the belly of the instrument.

Cases

1. If spring clips are used to hold the bows, be certain that they are not weak or bent. This will prevent the top of the instrument from being scratched.
2. Request samples of bass covers before ordering because sizes vary.

Selecting a dealer: local or mail-order?

Music dealers are an important part of the educational process. Teachers should make every attempt to locate a full-service dealer in the area. Teachers and dealers must recognize each other's abilities and work in an atmosphere of mutual understanding and respect. Communication is the key to success. The educator should:

1. Plan as far ahead as possible.
2. Give the store a copy of the letter sent to parents regarding rental of instruments.
3. Give the store a list of required method books and accessories.
4. Inform the dealers when beginners will be obtaining instruments.
5. Discuss specific requirements with the dealer ahead of time.
6. Coordinate efforts with other schools as much as possible, especially in large districts.
7. Let dealers know what is expected of them, and listen to what they expect of teachers.

Music dealers can be strong supporters of your program in the community. They provide immediate access to music, accessories, and repair service. As a matter of professional ethics, educators should not act as selling agents but should let the dealers handle the financial arrangements.

Music dealers can provide many fringe benefits for the string program. These include loaner instruments plus folders, posters, films, brochures, and other promotional materials. An education-oriented dealer cannot stay in business if teachers use their services but do not conduct any business with them. It is mutually advantageous for dealers and teachers to work together successfully.

Concepts in purchasing

The first step: Consultations with either local or mail-order companies prior to purchasing necessary musical equipment is the most important ingredient in making the correct purchasing decision. Dealing with a knowledgeable vendor who has experience and product expertise is necessary to secure the best and most reliable equipment for the least money.

How to save money: There are often numerous brands with little or no measurable difference between them. Knowledge is therefore critical when making an evaluation. Clearly, stretching the budget is too often a matter of survival, and to overlook an area of savings would be negligent. All purchases, however, must comply with specifications. (There is, of course, a point of diminishing returns. There is no savings if the instrument is so poorly adjusted or produces such an inadequate tone that the student becomes discouraged and drops out.)

More savings: Another way to save money is to inquire before ordering or placing a bid about the availability of nonpackaged-deal outfits. Sometimes purchases of complete outfits may be more costly than purchasing components that the string specialist has recommended. Do not limit yourself to a single brand. You may be overlooking equal or superior instruments and accessories that, if tested, would offer excellent quality and service. The lowest price is not necessarily a savings, but a reasonable price for a good-quality product is. Poor quality and a wide variety of mixed products in poor stages of adjustment, such as poorly matched strings, pegs, and fine tuners can present problems that may interfere with instruction. Use discretion.

Experience counts: Experienced personnel should be available for questions and advice before and after the sale. Mail-order firms and local dealers must be able to competently discuss pros and cons of any item in their catalog or store inventory.

Repair

Minor accidents to instruments are unavoidable and, because of their high frequency, teachers should become familiar with making necessary minor repairs. Major repairs are best left to professionals and, considering the size limitations of mail or shipping services, cellos and basses are best repaired locally. One can get repair advice from a local repair shop or by calling the toll-free number of a mail-order stringed instrument dealer. It is in the best interest of teachers and schools to encourage attendance at various workshops and seminars that are offered in the area of minor repairs and adjustments of stringed instruments (see "Training string teachers," pages 14-18).

Try samples

Regardless of your string supplier's location relative to the school site, it is prudent to request samples of the products you are considering. The string staff should have a hands-on opportunity to evaluate any product before making a purchase. Also, samples are often available at prices lower than bids since they offer the supplier product exposure.

Quality–dependability–price–selection–customer service: Find a local or long-distance music supplier who offers all of the above. Purchases and repairs will be more reasonably priced and more reliable when these services are available.

APPENDIX

Photo by John Froelich

Nomenclature

- Tip
- Head
- Scroll
- Peg
- Pegbox
- String nut
- Hair
- Fingerboard
- Neck
- Stick
- Top
- Upper bout
- "C" bout
- Soundpost (inside)
- Bridge
- F hole
- Tailpiece
- Lower bout
- Winding
- Chin rest
- Thumb leather
- Tailgut
- Ferrule ring
- Saddle
- Frog
- Endbutton
- Slide
- Screw button

VIOLIN OR VIOLA AND BOW

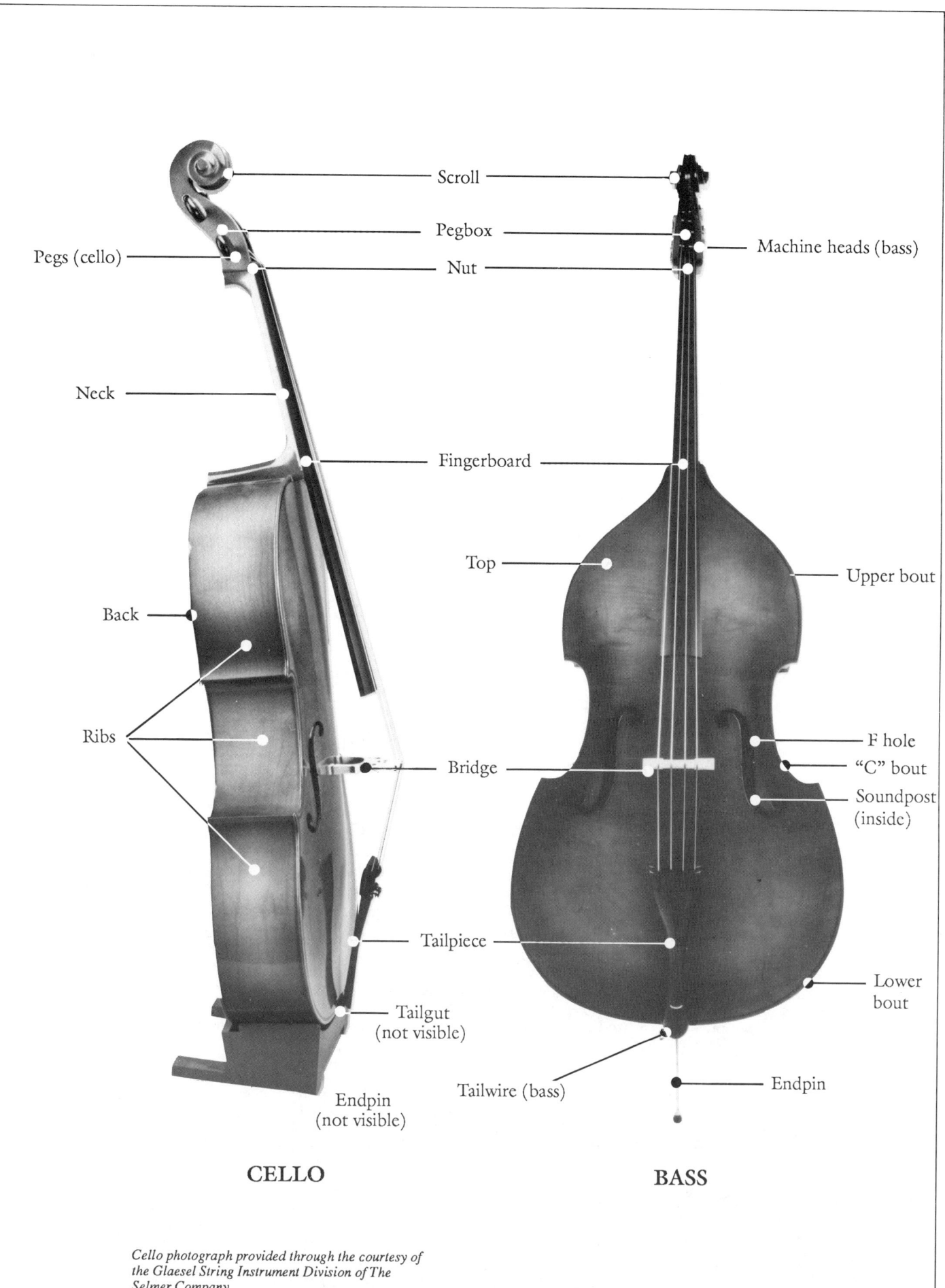

Cello photograph provided through the courtesy of the Glaesel String Instrument Division of The Selmer Company.

STRINGED INSTRUMENT SIZE CHART

(All lengths are given in inches.)

Size	Overall Length	Body Length	Vibrating String Length	Bow Length
Violin:				
4/4*	23 1/8	14	12 13/16	29 1/8
3/4*	21 5/8	13 1/4	12	27
1/2	20 3/8	12 3/8	11 5/16	24 1/4
Suzuki violin:				
1/4	18 3/5	11 1/4	10 3/8	22 3/8
1/8	17	10	9 1/4	19 1/8
1/10	15 1/2	9 1/4	8 3/8	19 1/8
1/16	14 1/4	8 1/4	7 5/8	17
Viola:				
Junior*	21 5/8	13 1/4	12	27
Interm.*	23 1/8	14	12 13/16	29 1/8
15	25 1/4	15	13 5/8	29 1/8
15 1/2	26 1/16	15 1/2	14 5/16	29 1/8
16	26 1/2	16	14 3/8	29 1/8
16 1/2	27 3/8	16 1/2	14 7/8	29 1/8
Cello:				
4/4	48 1/4	29 5/8	27 1/8	28 3/16
3/4	44 3/8	27 3/8	24 1/2	27
1/2	41 1/2	25 1/2	22 15/16	25 3/4
Suzuki cello:				
1/2	38	24	21 5/8	25 3/4
1/4	33 1/2	21	18 7/8	20 1/4
1/8	29	17 7/8	16 1/2	20 1/4
1/10	26 1/4	16	14 5/8	18 3/8
Bass:†				
4/4	74 1/2	45 1/2	43 1/8	Standard French 28 3/4
3/4 (std)	72 1/2	42 1/2	40 5/8	Standard Butler/German 29 3/4
1/2	65 1/2	40	37 3/8	Junior French 26 1/2
				Junior Butler/German 27 7/8

*A 3/4 violin and a junior viola are the same length. In addition, a 4/4 violin is the same length as an intermediate viola.

†4/4 or 7/8 size basses are used only for professional orchestra players. They are not suitable for school use.

Note: All measurements are approximate. The body length determines the size of the instrument. It is measured from the top shoulder (upper edge where the neck joins the body) to the end of the lower bout (base of the instrument). Standard bass bows are used for 3/4 and 4/4 basses. Junior bass bows are used for 1/2 size and smaller size basses.

SUMMARY OF INSTRUMENT MATERIALS AND CONSTRUCTION

Materials:
1. Back, sides, and scroll should be made of matched, quartered maple, loft seasoned for at least seven years.
2. The top should be of quartered, mountain-grown spruce, even grained and loft seasoned for at least seven years.
3. Backs should be carved maple and graduated. The carved top should be of quarter-cut spruce.

   Note: Some instruments have pressed tops, which may be acceptable for basic student violins. Some inexpensive models also have "painted" purfling instead of genuine inlaid purfling. These instruments, if well adjusted, may also be suitable for beginning students.

4. The scroll and neck should be carved from hard maple.
5. The sides should be bent from solid maple strips that match the back and scroll.
6. The lining and corner blocks as well as the upper and lower blocks should be of spruce, willow, or poplar.
7. The soundpost and the bass bar should be of seasoned spruce.
8. The bridge should be of seasoned and quartered maple.
9. The pegs, fingerboard, string nut, saddle, and tailpiece should be ebony.
10. Laminated maple backs and sides and laminated spruce tops are acceptable for beginner cellos and basses; however, they should never be accepted on violins and violas.

Construction:
1. Tops and backs should be carved, preferably from two pieces of matching spruce and maple. The top and back plates should be graduated.
2. The rib structure should have four solid, well-fitting corner blocks as well as upper and lower blocks.
3. The ribs should have a full set of linings around the edge of the top as well as around the edge of the back.
4. The bass bar should be fitted into the top from a separate piece of spruce.
5. The top and back should be securely glued around the entire edge with violin maker's glue (hot glue).
6. All carved instruments should be purfled with "inlaid" purfling. (Laminated tops and back should not be purfled, since edges chip more easily.)
7. Necks should be fitted at the proper angle, snugly fitted, and well glued.

8. Fingerboard, pegs, tailpiece, bridge, and soundpost should be fitted and properly adjusted in the United States to ensure proper playing.
9. The finish should be smooth, handrubbed violin varnish. Spirit varnishes are commonly used on student-line instruments; better instruments should be finished with oil varnish. (Lacquer finishes are not acceptable.)
10. Necks, fingerboards, and bridges should never be covered with varnish or lacquer. Necks should be stained and oil treated or French polished.
11. Strings may be made of steel, chrome-wound-on-gut, or a synthetic core like nylon or perlon. Strings should be of good quality, fresh, and properly matched.
12. An adjustable, threaded, nylon-type material is best for tailpieces made of wood. Metal or nylon loops are used for metal tailpieces, and brass wire or cable is used only on basses.